D1223304

Ragdolls Are the Best!

Elaine Landau

LERNER PUBLICATIONS COMPANY • MINNEAPOLIS

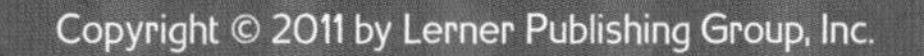

Lerner Publications Company
A division of Lerner Publishing Group, Inc.
241 First Avenue North
Minneapolis, MN 55401 U.S.A.

Website address: www.lernerbooks.com

Library of Congress Cataloging-in-Publication Data

Landau, Elaine.
Ragdolls are the best! / by Elaine Landau.
p. cm. — (The best cats ever)
Includes index.
ISBN 978-0-7613-6428-3 (lib. bdg. : alk. paper)
1. Ragdoll cat—Juvenile literature. I. Title.
SF449.R34L36 2011
636.8'3–dc22 2010016848

Manufactured in the United States of America
1 - CG - 12/31/10

TABLE OF CONTENTS

CHAPTER ONE

WHAT A DOLL!

I'm thinking of a special cat. This fine feline is not like most other cats. It's more like a big hunk of love on four feet. It's gentle, loyal, and very sweet. It's fun and friendly too. But you'd expect that. I'm talking about a **ragdoll**.

A ragdoll relaxes in its owner's arms.

Why are these cute kitties called ragdolls? Pick one up, and you'll see. They really relax in your arms. Their bodies become limp and floppy. It's like holding a rag doll.

A Great Big Beauty

Ragdolls are not itty-bitty kitties. They are big-boned beauties. The average house cat weighs from 6 to 15 pounds (3 to 7 kilograms). But ragdolls can weigh as much as 20 pounds (9 kg). Male ragdolls are usually a bit larger than females.

The Name Game

Ragdolls are super cats. And every super cat needs a super name. Do any of these fit your pretty kitty?

Flopsey
Lovey
BLUEBELL
Zeus
Dolly
Ann
Sweetie Pie
Venus
Andy
Hamlet

A Sight to See

Ragdolls have fluffy, medium-length coats and bushy tails. Their fur is soft and silky. It's a lot like a bunny rabbit's. Ragdolls have big blue eyes to boot. What a great combination!

Famous Hotel Cat

In the late 1930s, a cat wandered into the Algonquin Hotel in New York City. The hotel's owner welcomed the cat. He let it live at the hotel. Ever since, a cat has lived under the roof of the Algonquin. The cat that lives there these days is a ragdoll.

The kitty's name is Matilda *(right)*, and the guests just love her. Each year, the hotel throws Matilda a big birthday bash. Usually more than one hundred of her closest friends attend. She's one special ragdoll!

Colorful Kitties

Ragdolls are pointed cats. But don't worry. This doesn't mean their heads or tails are pointed! It just means that some areas—or "points"—on their bodies are darker than others. The darker areas are on or near the cats' ears, faces, legs, and tails.

A ragdoll's points come in different colors. Their points can be any of these six colors:

- seal (dark brown)
- cream (sandy brown to yellowish white)
- lilac (pinkish beige)
- blue (a shade of gray)
- red (reddish orange)
- chocolate (the color of a milk chocolate bar)

Ragdolls' bodies are usually ivory, beige, white, or gray. They also have different patterns in addition to the points. These may include stripes or light shading.

This is a red-pointed ragdoll.

This ragdoll is a blue point.

A Super Pal

Most ragdolls adore their owners. These cats love being held and petted. Ragdolls are also smart. They can learn some tricks and are quite playful. Their owners think they are the best cats ever!

CHAPTER TWO

HOW THE BREED GOT STARTED

Think of California. Do sun, sand, and surf come to mind? You probably didn't think of ragdoll cats. But that's where this beautiful breed got its start.

Ragdolls got their start in California.

It all began in the early 1960s. A cat breeder named Ann Baker spotted an unusual cat in her neighborhood. The cat was called Josephine. She was large and white. She had long hair and pretty blue eyes.

The large white cat in this photo may be Josephine. Ann Baker took the photo in the 1960s.

Alone and on Her Own

But things weren't going well for Josephine. She was homeless and on her own. Ann quickly saw that this cat was special. Josephine was very sweet and gentle.

Ann Baker bred Josephine with this male cat. His name was Daddy Warbucks.

Ann took Josephine in and cared for her. Ann soon bred Josephine with a male cat. Ann hoped the kittens would be as special as their mother.

Josephine had a litter of terrific kittens. They were blue-eyed and beautiful. They were also as sweet as sugar!

Ann Baker poses with one of her first litters of ragdolls. The kittens' names were (from left to right) Kookie, Toy Sue, and Kookie Tu.

Cats Among the Ancient Romans

The ancient Romans found cats useful. They hunted mice and rats. They were also kept as pets. Cats did well at both these jobs.

This ancient Roman mosaic (a picture made of small tiles) shows a tabby cat and some ducks.

Cats in Ancient Egypt

The ancient Egyptians worshipped cats. Their goddess Bast had a woman's body and a cat's head. No one was allowed to take a cat out of ancient Egypt or kill a cat. Those who did risked being put to death.

A statue of Bast, the cat-headed Egyptian goddess

The Birth of the Best Breed Ever

Ann Baker knew that she'd hit on something wonderful. As time passed, she kept breeding Josephine. She bred her kittens too.

All the new cats were large and good looking. They were also smart, playful, and easygoing. They were the start of the ragdoll breed.

Ragdolls are playful cats. They enjoy exploring their surroundings.

That's the ragdoll story. These fancy felines didn't come from the palaces of Europe. They can't be traced to the deserts of the Middle East either. It all started with a stray cat from California. But what a cat!

CHAPTER THREE

SO YOU REALLY WANT A RAGDOLL

You feel that you've just got to have a ragdoll. You want it more than extra birthday money. You'd even trade your new Wii game for one.

Wait! Don't rush out to get a ragdoll. Ragdolls may seem like purr-fect pets. But they aren't right for everyone.

An Indoor Cat

Do you think of cats as outdoor pets? Think again—especially if you want a ragdoll. Roaming outdoors is dangerous for any cat. Cats can be hit by cars or eat things that might make them sick. And ragdolls are just too sweet and friendly to be left on their own outdoors. They might not defend themselves against animals that could hurt them. If your family can't commit to having an indoor pet, you shouldn't get a ragdoll.

Ragdolls are safest when they are kept indoors.

Do You Really Want a Clingy Cat?

Ragdolls live on love. Your cat will always want to be with you. Do you like to watch TV? Like to do your homework on your bed? Don't count on doing these things by yourself. Your ragdoll will be right there with you. Your cat may even try to follow you into the bathroom!

Ragdolls love to be around their owners. Be prepared for company!

Would you like having a ragdoll as your shadow? Or would you rather have an independent cat? Think about these things before adopting a ragdoll.

Ragdolls are very social cats. They enjoy snuggling with people as well as other animals.

A Good Choice

Ragdolls make wonderful family members. They do well with children as well as older people. They tend to get along with other household pets. These cats love having company over. Often they will greet your guests at the door!

Ragdolls are also not for people who aren't home much. Do you have lots of activities after school? Are you always out of the house on weekends? If so, pass on getting a ragdoll. You'll have a very lonely kitty.

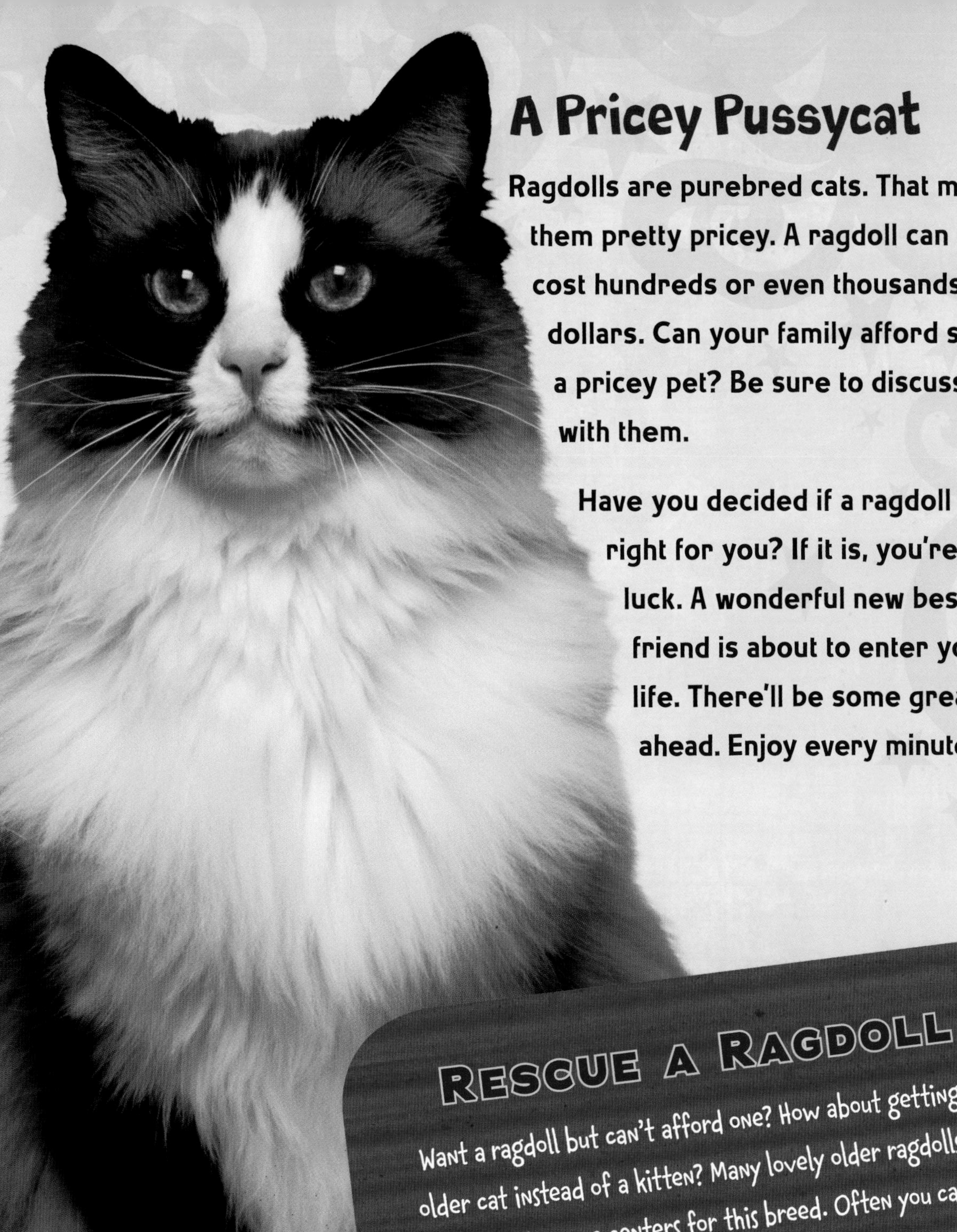

A Pricey Pussycat

Ragdolls are purebred cats. That makes them pretty pricey. A ragdoll can cost hundreds or even thousands of dollars. Can your family afford such a pricey pet? Be sure to discuss this with them.

Have you decided if a ragdoll is right for you? If it is, you're in luck. A wonderful new best friend is about to enter your life. There'll be some great fun ahead. Enjoy every minute of it!

Rescue a Ragdoll

Want a ragdoll but can't afford one? How about getting an older cat instead of a kitten? Many lovely older ragdolls are available at rescue centers for this breed. Often you can get one for a low fee. Just remember: All cats are expensive. Even if you don't pay much for your new pet, your family will still need to spend money on food and health care. But adopting a rescue cat *can* help you cut down on the purchase price.

CHAPTER FOUR

WELCOME YOUR RAGDOLL

What a day! It could be the best day of your life. You're bringing home your ragdoll.

Get Ready

Make this a great day for your ragdoll too. Be sure you have everything you need for your new cat. Buy it some basic supplies. Here's a starter list of things you'll need:

- food and water bowls
- cat food
- litter box
- kitty litter
- brush and wide-tooth steel comb
- scratching post
- cat carrier

Get Kitty to a Vet

Take your ragdoll to a veterinarian soon. That's a doctor who takes care of animals. They are called vets for short.

A veterinarian holds a kitten. Veterinarians treat both dogs and cats as well as other animals.

The vet will check your pet's health. Your ragdoll will also get the shots it needs to stay healthy. Take your cat back to the vet for checkups. And take your cat to the vet right away if it gets sick.

This vet makes sure her furry patient is healthy.

It's Feeding Time

Ask your vet what to feed your cat. Don't give your pet extra snacks. If you have an ice-cream cone, don't share it with your kitty. A fat cat is an unhealthy animal. A ragdoll is a big cat—but it shouldn't look like a baby elephant!

Ice cream might be a tasty treat for you, but it isn't good for cats.

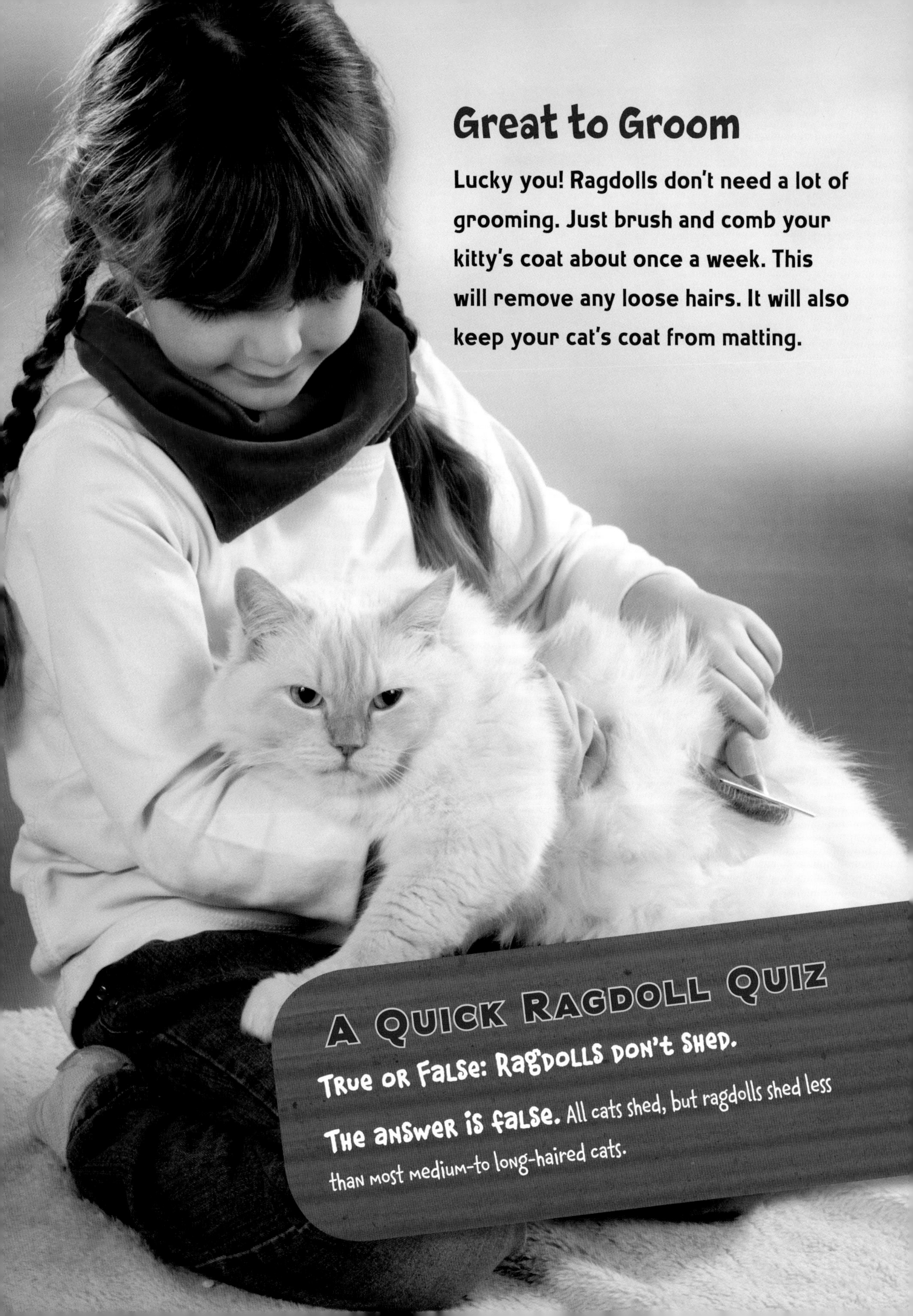

Great to Groom

Lucky you! Ragdolls don't need a lot of grooming. Just brush and comb your kitty's coat about once a week. This will remove any loose hairs. It will also keep your cat's coat from matting.

A Quick Ragdoll Quiz

True or False: Ragdolls don't shed.

The answer is false. All cats shed, but ragdolls shed less than most medium-to long-haired cats.

You and Your Ragdoll

Your ragdoll will love you and always be there for you. To your cat, you're a rock star! So be the best pet owner you can be.

Take good care of your cat, even when you're busy or tired. You'll be glad you did. A ragdoll is a great pal!

Is That Cat Part Dog?

How are ragdolls like dogs? These cats often follow their owners from room to room. Most also like to play fetch. Throw a small ball to your cat, and have a ball together!

GLOSSARY

breed: a particular type of cat. Cats of the same breed have the same body shape and general features. The word *breed* can also refer to mating cats to produce kittens.

breeder: someone who mates cats to produce a particular type of cat

coat: a cat's fur

feline: a cat or having to do with cats

groom: to clean, brush, and trim a cat's coat

matting: severe tangling. Matting causes fur to clump together in large masses.

pointed: to have dark areas of fur. Pointed cats have dark fur on or near their ears, faces, legs, and tails.

purebred: a cat whose parents are of the same breed

rescue center: a shelter where stray and abandoned cats are kept until they are adopted

shed: to lose fur

stray: a homeless cat

veterinarian: a doctor who treats animals. Veterinarians are called vets for short.

FOR MORE INFORMATION

Books

Brecke, Nicole, and Particia M. Stockland. *Cats You Can Draw*. Minneapolis: Millbrook Press, 2010. Perfect for cat lovers, this colorful book teaches readers how to draw many popular cat breeds, including the ragdoll.

Brown, Ruth. *Gracie the Lighthouse Cat*. London: Anderson Press, 2011. Gracie the lighthouse cat and Grace Darling, the lighthouse keeper's daughter, both have an adventure one very windy night.

Harris, Trudy. *Tally Cat Keeps Track*. Minneapolis: Millbrook Press, 2011. Tally McNally is a cat who loves to tally—but one day, he gets into a jam. Will his friends find a way to help him?

Stevens, Kathryn. *Cats*. Mankato, MN: Child's World, 2009. Stevens offers a basic guide to cat care.

Stone, Lynn M. *Ragdoll Cats*. Vero Beach, FL: Rourke, 2010. Stone describes the ragdoll cat's personality and provides a history of the breed.

Websites

ASPCA Kids

http://www.aspca.org/aspcakids

Check out this website for helpful hints on caring for a cat and other pets.

For Kids: About Cats

http://kids.cfa.org

Be sure to visit this website for kids on cats and cat shows. Don't miss the link to some fun games as well.

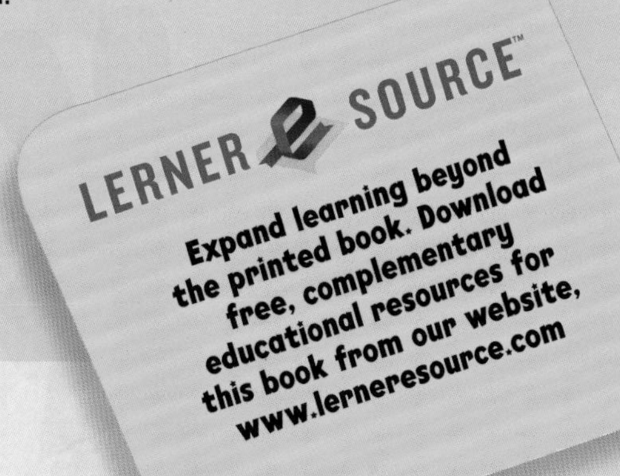

Index

Photo Acknowledgments

The images in this book are used with the permission of: backgrounds © iStockphoto.com/javarman3 and © iStockphoto.com/Julie Fisher; © iStockphoto.com/Michael Balderas, p. 1; © Marc Henire/Dorling Kindersley/Getty Images, pp. 4-5, 6-7; © Linn Currie/Shutterstock Images, pp. 5, 10, 18; © Eric Isselée/Dreamstime.com, p. 6 (top); AP Photo/Jennifer Szymaszek, p. 6 (bottom); © Juniors Bildarchiv/Alamy, pp. 7, 15; © Linncurrie/Dreamstime.com, pp. 8 (left), 22; © Hanna Monika Cybulko/Dreamstime.com, p. 8 (right); © Dave Wetzel/Dreamstime.com, p. 9; Wain Pearce, pp. 11 (top), 12 (both); © Studio Paggy/Getty Images, p. 11 (bottom); © SuperStock/SuperStock, p. 13 (top); © The Art Gallery Collection/Alamy, p. 13 (bottom); © ARDEA/LABAT, JEAN MICHEL/Animals Animals, pp. 14-15; © Dave King/Dorling Kindersley/Getty Images, p. 16; © Yves Lanceau/NHPA/Photoshot, p. 17; AP Photo/Vadim Ghirda, p. 19 (top); © NaturePL/SuperStock, p. 19 (bottom); © Petra Wegner/Alamy, p. 20; © GK Hart/Vikki Hart/Photodisc/Getty Images, p. 21; © Mark Bond/Dreamstime.com, p. 23 (top right); © Eti Swinford/Dreamstime.com, p. 23 (center right); © iStockphoto.com/Jennifer Sheets, p. 23 (bottom right); © Agita Leimane/Dreamstime.com, p. 23 (bottom left); © Ariel Skelley/Riser/Getty Images, p. 24; © Thomas Barwick/Lifesize/Getty Images, p. 25; © Ulrike Schanz Fotodesign, pp. 26 (left), 27, 28, 29; © Comstock Images/Getty Images, p. 26 (right); © GK Hart/Vikki Hart/Brand X Pictures/Getty Images, pp. 28-29.

Front cover: © Geoffrey Robinson/Alamy.
Back cover: © Tony Campbell/Dreamstime.com.